Refuge
and Occasion

Refuge
and Occasion

Vyt Bakaitis

Station Hill Press

BARRYTOWN, NY

Published by Station Hill Press, the publishing project of the Institute for Publishing Arts, Inc., 120 Station Hill Road, Barrytown, NY 12507, New York, a not-for-profit, tax-exempt organization [501(c)(3)].

Online catalogue: www.stationhill.org

e-mail: publishers@stationhill.org

Cover image: Ron Gorchov, *2nd Study: Gift of the Naxions* (2011) gouache drawing, 9 × 7.75 inches (6/11). In the author's collection.

Cover and interior design: Susan Quasha

Library of Congress Cataloging-in-Publication Data

Names: Bakaitis, Vyt, 1940- author.
Title: Refuge & occasion / Vyt Bakaitis.
Other titles: Refuge and occasion
Description: Barrytown, NY : Station Hill Press, [2021] |
Identifiers: LCCN 2021044098 | ISBN 9781581772111 (trade paperback)
Subjects: LCGFT: Poetry.
Classification: LCC PS3552.A3947 R44 2022 | DDC 811/.54—dc23
LC record available at https://lccn.loc.gov/2021044098

For my friends
William Benton
&
George Quasha

makers
& doers
both

Contents

Refuge
and Occasion

Lapse into Recovery

But it's not as if it should all be black
at least in the heart of the oval mirror

Stern refuge finer than flimsiest dust
in the unlanced somnolence of an airy bubble

How the brow overhangs your eyes as a shading
leaf leaves the tree with no singular claim

A sunkissed souvenir takes on the glow
drenched to accompany thunder

Lightning now cuts loose a shudder
of crushed foil to take away at eye level

Paraclete

In the land of enchantments,
everyone has a story

The arena we live in whispers collide
no dream without exaggeration is rumor-free

In the night it is always night and just because
no uncertified arguments ever set us free

So long as we keep worrying
guidelines we do so love reshaping

Planes have fallen from the sky
and our people were on them

Cars pile up a monument to distraction
to shake free of the least secret claim

Trucking in full regalia one small clean failure
pitching in and missing for a low-slung ozone

Lifelines, after Artūras Jautakas

Thanks to all of you dear friends
   that you helped me to stand up
   that you helped to hold me up
   that you thought of me enough
   so I know not to give up
   any of the friends I've got

Thanks to all of you dear friends
   now I know you feel for me
   no overdose of polite pity
   and never brought me low enough
   to drown in sorrow deeper down
   where peace yields to oblivion

Thanks to all of you dear friends
   for keeping me from any intent
   to cry out in despair
   whenever you're not near
   with real hope for a new life
   to rouse our future into cheer

Votive

No mountain has stood as I have stood
in line for the cashier at the corner market
next to tubs cramped with flowers on ice

While birds are scarce this January
their agility outpacing each shadow
only a jetlagged pair of sparrows
keeps pondering the pavement

That yesterday maybe cleared a place
for us here though it may have been
before then the days began to lag

Long before a cold truth can assert itself
past the dawn when everything's woven
into a vaguely significant distance

Small incentive
happenstance

Abiding Faith, at the Solstice

We don't need a breeze to tell us
        there's life in the trees

All stand the test of time
        alone with their pins or leaves

And need none of the names we give them
        to do as they please

Acting like so many children
        ignoring our pleas

Should the snows crowd in they'll still
        hold still and
        remember not to freeze

And each has a reason to stay wherever
        regardless how far from the sun

Given time each one keels over
        with a hope the green will return

From the Lithuanian

Standing on top of a stump
I watched for stars

Cold wind kicked the dark
into my eyes

Sending the song of a gloomy pine grove
down to sleeping humankind

Could that be death come down to earth
along with the last gleam of light?

A boy wrote this
because he couldn't sleep

Alone so lonely
dead to the world before he could dream
any future he'd claim was his

Now I think of him nearing death
so many years since
I wish I could sleep

Stone Pit

It's merely a pebble from the road
but why did I stoop to pick this one
still is an open question

I don't need to describe
it to you, no gift was
intended, but the feel
of it in my hand, small
as it was for my palm
to close down on and have
it nest there, close
so I could feel something

Vital, but without thought
of possession, except it held
all my attention until
I no longer could see where I was
nor knew what to think
any more than I can
blink away stars
caught in the clamp
down brilliance
the nighttime brings

Has fireflies
spell out their wild
scrawl hint of a whim
could it be the pattern
to inform this experience?

How Absence Commences

There was the moment he wanted to preserve the look she had before both turned away. But the last thing he saw on rounding the corner was the guy she was with spit on the sidewalk.

Still his own mind could track back to the times he'd seen her before that he could still remember. Most of those times she'd be walking towards him, instead of away. And he looked long, still does, and now that she's gone, can still see her, but all too distant, and it's not the same.

"It's been real" was the last thing she said.

"And now the absence begins," all he could stammer.

It was late in the day, the sun directly behind him, and even after he'd gone the many blocks it took for her image to retreat and fade, his feet kept trying to pin down a full shadow at each step.

The Power

is not an
exacting
language

but a gasp
that holds
to no clue

before a just
coaxing summons
brings on

exception
to every
set rule

My verbs don't have
the dignity to make
a move my nerves
don't dare show
or make jokes
even after the
laughs I can't
join in words
are about and
can't hold to
that essential

A push for a pulse
from here to haste
a blindspot thrust
the moment's trepidation
quivering before it goes
for all you know to show

You
free of a breath's lease

High as the sky
is the place I remember
    the wild wave struck before we could rally against it
    so even losing count of the few of us there all before
    we could think to prepare we might possibly be survivors
    since we had our minds set and not a moment to hang on to

what could we care to welcome

the house no longer standing

a mudhole wipeout

though the sky helps
widen the highway
striving for air

After Parmenides, *pace* Charles Stein
                                    my head wasn't
spinning when I started darn stubborn
                                        mule but I saw the wheels
had a light the color in bands reeling
                                    backwards some entrancing
circles to overwhelm my longing
                                    straining to stay on track
so that I wished I knew

where I was heading a blinding resplendence
grinding in my ears
swells a rousing fresh allure the young girls
just drop
their filtering veils to a glowing ember
in winter as if
daylight isn't sure the darkness can yield
any light
I'm framed inside
behind mighty doors
the terms being dealt favor could swing
either way and so melt the keys
to seal off a whole

new lifeline before its history

opens to reveal a dream

young as the storming moment

a voice beyond the reach of years

By the loose ribbon her hair makes
whoever might dare to claim her
   will need to redeem her

though she said that and
   it seemed to be true
the waiting was more than
   a full measure of home

For the Musicke

To begin in the simplest way
as if I had something to say

Or to find the plain word
I may have overheard

Otillia
my
Otillia

You are the Muse
    every sound I hear
    has midnight stars
    daylight bright
not to disperse

Your smile rings a cheer
will not disappear

So let it be her shoulder
or twirl of a hip
in the laminate cloud
above the skyline
I've seen from the beach
at Nice

And leave imagining
so understated
it's best expressed
remedial to last
the human day
en masse

Way before

she got there

⌐

All wanderings
since childhood
may claim only
a stopover

short on sleep
sort of where
it only leads
to catch up

⌐

Even in sleep why are
things familiar names
never heard of here
secure in a dream
before it's over

Under the heavy
pillow of sleep

You made me love you
I am not the same

More than you think
less than I know

Let the gods puzzle over
what makes it so

Less than you think
more than I know

Days pile up
only to shrink

For the moment
so I can't think

In the waiting room
remind me for a bit
the plants all had leaves
like tongues sticking out
that you said you knew
what mad season it was
I had to wonder still do
for so many days
over the years

~

We were in our last year
high school then a twilight
       décor the only kind
       we were sure gave
a clue we got used to
slow music the horns
       cars cruising by
       on the way back
locked in exhaust
back from the drive-in

~

Funny now to think
how later that year
we had no plan
to fix on or
pitch into
I thought you looked
going in for the test
so accomplished
you'd only a game
ahead to think of
but not the game
you ever could
give yourself to

~

In your eyes the most
fluttering part of you

not the eyes I think of
dreaming and framed in
each entrance you made

I could at once be part of
just being there to see it

Your pulse tuned to a music
I almost know by heart

Epilog

Death. Death. Death.
Posted as the last words
Gandhi is said to have spoken

Wealth
without work
has no cushion

The Mahatma
a public servant
was puzzling over
Cartier-Bresson's
                    photo of two elderly
                    ladies frowning in
                    self-evident dismay
before he
          stepped out
to get
        shot

Thought without feeling
has no face

Pleasure without beauty
brings no privilege

Work without play
runs to waste

Without conscience
it's all nonsense

Man Listening to Mozart, Robert Scull in Memory

Feel free to breathe easy
though the urge is there

To speak out more than
feeling alone

The longing
beyond words

A lunge at rushhour
for the first available cab

Late Stepping Stones

Days have so shrunk
as though stuck
on icefloes

And everywhere
winter goes
you stay

Not far behind
stranded and
riled

How can I trust you
to be wise when
you've run out of words
as the river flows

Birthdays follow the clown
crowned on a far horizon
trying to make
his case known
after sundown

Sparklers outshine the stars
while the big wheel
still spins
sawdust swept up
between the acts

When and if ever
will we grow
weary of war
as we know it
when will it wear
us down to the nub
of a ridiculous
if no less than
frivolous
existence

Owed to the Future

Now the sun shines fierce
on our swollen earth
there's no time to reverse
what ages prolonged hard labor
is about to bring to birth

Whole harvests nearing year's end
rate fewer voices to cheer the trend
while our feel for the future cues up a clear danger
with no star to guide us from market to manger

Let's lower the lunar lamp
to redefine our swamp

Extend our fond tradition
of a gifting competition
and occupy ourselves
for a global show of common sense
so love and peace light up the skies

Let anxiety soak in the wintry brine
to ripen to a premise the promise
on the shield you wear
cheeky rouge

Solstice Salute

Praise the sun, sure core
for the glow to spark
each day and then some

Praise the sun, for warmth
it brings a kindness but
the balance we need to address

Praise the sun, stay warm
in friendship but not vex
with burns nor stun with floods

Praise the sun, but be warned
what's going down is
all our own making

Praise the sun, that our clocks
not run down or dull
a luminous chime

Praise the sun, though it
retreats from the beach
where children still play

Praise the sun, even when
night shimmers brighter
than a daytime scan

Praise the sun, for every
inch of garden it allows
anywhere in the world

Praise the sun, for no less
than each tree unfolds
the promise of return

Some Life in Poetry

I shot a sparrow on a dare
with a flurry it rose then dropped

I felt nowhere so dead scared
ever to touch a BB gun again

Strange all I found and still carry
what I remember left me to wonder

The huge outdoor factory clock held out
no promise to my view a clear alarming

War drone right at noon where I stood
for some time it was more than human

On second thought I'd had enough
from reading into it more than I should

I sat on a bench with a phantom
when it was all I desired the leaf

Each sunset wore a cliché of colors
but then I met her who let

The sun stun us out of the blue
and change the face of each day

Words come they're not mine

but will show where I've been

And before I knew it I was dead
certain never to go back again

Asleep or waking
but for the singing still around

First to Last

Open on blue
how a boy can
stand owl-eyed
transfixed before
the woman laid-out
on the bier had one
glass eye kept open
and so staring blue

Dig down and sing
to where the sheer
wave-lashed piers
prowl and awaken
their menace walk
along for a sound
smothered blast

Dig deep and sing
right to the core
but never to lose
once in a while
let memory snag
the living proof
won't let go

O sing me unalone
not for a lullaby
let morning come

unsnarled and ripen
with love to last
in each held breath
measured as new
beyond dreams

All is alive
and everything
is enough

A Causeway Tract. The First Indictment

You stand in the rubble
waiting for nightfall
to diminish the blemish
you're building
                        under construction is
                        what the rubble's from

In the swim by nature
dunked twice and then
let your name come up
not the same and yet
here least expected
                        before sighting land
                        all eyes turn to scan
                        the spread dead ahead

Your name trips from our lips
such staggering fragments
fester a while in a round
whirlwind curdling curses
the blood of your strained estate
an inane bestiality scorned into words
by any other name is unsalvageable drivel
                                    you were not the first to exhaust
                                    and yet endorse in fact you're the
                                    front-runner caught in a tailwind
from a blizzard of blown opportunities
a gross malignancy on the growth
of your self-alleged authentic

will leave a wet spot
from the meltdown on
the ground you stain

Though you let rage build to a squall
and build a seawall to restrain the flood
extend brute piers to sway where a harbor
swerves to confine the surging purge
so let it gleam into a brimming
expansion a row of icicles lined up
like chipped tooth knock-offs
where the sun hit

You may want too much
though it's not enough
to quell the stubborn
nag of inbred distemper
you feel that moves you
to buy favors outright
chase after and drain away
all there is for the gain

some woman you come on to
the women come with a price
far above what fame exposes
never to reclaim much
composure as such

But for all the fuss you will
let your children plot
and kill for
what they've not got

and not just because
it's all temporary
only and always
as is

Enough is enough
can't let you play
the menacing Beast
Lock you up snug
in a Hall of Mirrors
throw the key away
Strike the clock
from noon to none
do time your way
A live tombstone
your feet in cement
do it now we can't wait

In the book of consequence
let your name be inscribed
with a dull knife on clear glass
with a blunt brick on broken glass
with a flurry of dead feathers
in a rushed mudslide
a chilling wind
to absolve
you absolutely
sheer acid rain

The Fact of You

So many road signs to the unforeseen

Now no one will know
what our time might have been

What do I or can I even begin to think
now where you've gone leaves no clue

Memory only gets me this far
the papers kept piling up for days

But when my heart stops
will I have gone the distance?

Earlier Last Month

Our traffic lanes, sidewalks too many
leaves snagged, though not all were
cleared by the time ploughs came
rumbling early last month
after the lush first snowfall
even before the hurricane
had drained entirely away

Where the hands touch
to be swept back

A leafless tree carves its shade
to hide the silence

Let our eyes
work the night
trying to make out
a fine print
in the stars

The First Sign of True Beauty

after Nicola Di Bari and Mogol

I strum on the guitar strings
       I have no time to play
       a sounder tune for you
       to try and make it stay
       so you won't turn away

Though I can't find the words for
       what my heart wants to say
       I love I love I love you
       is the closest I can come to
       repeating night and day

With flowers now in blossom
       your perfume on the breeze
       my sigh can't rise to meet it
       no matter how I try
       I almost want to die

The first sign of true beauty
       to ever feel so right
       your loving smile gives my love life

One star above the treeline
       once darkness hides the day
       keeps my love set for you to stay

The voice you hear me sing in
        lifts straight up from the heart
        I love I love I love you
        is all it keeps repeating
        to make you feel like taking part
With flowers now in blossom
                        a first sign

The first sign of true beauty
        to ever feel just right
        your loving smile gives my love life

Lone star above the treeline
        once darkness blinds the day
        makes my love sure that you will stay

The voice you hear me sing in
        lifts straight up from the heart
        I love I love I love you
        is all it keeps repeating
        to make you feel like taking part
I pray you'll feel like taking part
                      right from the start

Beyond These Dreams

You say that you love me
　　　　and that would be true
If only you'd let me
　　　　get closer to you
Now the smiles you gave
　　　　are starting to fade
And hugs from afar
　　　　can't reach where you are

Some say the best kissing
　　　　grows out of pure wishing
But for all the many kisses
　　　　sprout from our wishes
Let's best not raise a false alarm
　　　　over the huge swarm
To be hauled entirely from
　　　　close calls and near misses

Though if each wish were a kiss
　　　　we'd be braised into bliss

　　　2.
It was good to see you
　　　　though I should have known
You'd assert yourself
　　　　to brush off kisses before long
So good to see you
　　　　even though we're far apart

And nowhere near to saying
        goodbye not just yet

        3.
I can't guess that you knew
        all you've put me through
As there should be no harm from
        any whim to roam at random
But if there are gods left in heaven
        to look down on how we're loving
It's best we just leave love to them

        4.
If our union is to spin a wheel
with spokes to converge on a core
arms like mine to reach to the rim

Yours outstretched to signal each turn
so this one ongoing spiraling merger
still churns the sea and runs seasons

As the same flood I swam in before I could stand
or knew any word of love or its mouth
of a cave where it came from

        5.
Now I know you deserve better
        there is no more I can give
To be loving you forever
        without equal time to live

While our days run by the numbers
       as the light begins to shift
With no more of the agony
       to be shared in every kiss
Downward to a darkness
       no dawn can aim to lift
Tomorrow brings on memory
       (so Dante says some place)
And no free ride to any clearing
       where lovers leave a trace

6.

Come to me in dreams
You will not find me sleeping
Come as you are and stay
Not just for the keeping

Another hour and then
We're not to meet again
For once upon a time
We have to cry and mean
We're not saying goodbye

7.

Love, let me learn
How our time is bound to end
Not what we'll be leaving for
But the means to be found

I dream of you with longing
Your smile is still the guide
To show a hint of promise
For the love no loss can hide

Scroll Emblem, for Ron Gorchov

Not parsed or lobbed
but shaped and fused
into a tense sun its sum
    makes the cave safe
as a ship on stalled waters
times curvature to catch
the live spark is liquid
it trickles a note of music
    into random orbit
for a calling far summons
to a featureless future
and having left order
    framed out to stake risk
the lines are naked to a flare
from a keen forge that's been
    one on one in regarding
each ghost face to face
mind testing truculence
    back of the blinds
response at each station
unassigned packaging
each febrile vibration
    holds scattering eyes
as bleak as effaced
in effect abandoned
    but leaving a trance
we can fold our aim
trusting to silence

its elegant vow
   in a blanched light
out of the woods
shed these words
   and submit
   to a summit
   all splendor

Real Fact

No, not the night of the big storm
that it's bound to come again

The loneliest I've been was driving due West
into the slow sunset out of Sault Ste Marie

That was the year I'd lost you
stock sold, like a total fiction, in my head

I wish I knew more

What's real is the fact

Ditto

Nors ir
nesu visai tikras
su sava kalba
tik   it's not just
                      where
                            it goes until
nutilo metro
atitolo svietas

it grows out, it goes on so
                              not much of
                              it shows

        ❧

Dog-eared was not
Dog-tagged not yet
                    we left & turned
Right
        till it stuck
with no one to stop us

We took what
We left with
            all we got

        ❧

No picture will do
                    for even if that is

                     all there is of you
No picture will do

    ❧

Let the clock tell what it shows
the first letter to be set at zero
even before you wore clothes

Not to let on how much of it's in
what you caught from a mixup of
language the swing to & fro

And not let it go

    ❧

"teh oo-h" to hear the child tell it = *die Uhr*
every time it sounds past a pendulum stroke

a vast distance that day exploded
while bound to the code diuternal

too many where some seventy years
later on you'd think no letter would come

but one from the French in the barn
where the horses were stabled to haul back

hay from harvest and the calm on the water
was lulling where the wheels stumbled over

ruts in mock cadence while they hummed
their own song for a faraway home

Where not to go was the road right
in front where the small gate
kept the ducks in
                    sheer brilliance
to bring on radiance transform
its dismal essential from some
basic misery

that is me

Flight Delay

I stayed put while I waited
but you were not where I wanted
what with your own dream to pursue

So close to touch was the feeling
your voice alone made real
the legend kept changing

Once by trial our trust broke in two
intuition kept the loss on appeal
so much more than we could renew

Riddling a Wild Surmise

If I listen long enough and only
to myself I'm sure I'll go crazy

But even if now for once I hold my breath
you know for sure where to find me

Listening to you makes for another story
though it's sure to end the same way

A mouthful of pebbles on the tongue
won't scale the pitch eager to reverberate

For still unheard bells to declare it's safe
to assume we have some song in common

Continuity Factor

Let's pull out some maps. There are none
            nor can there be of the river itself
            Heraclitus says if time is the river

It flows freely unstaunched
        as only memory can
        deliberately cutting through
        to retrieve advance or forestall

Not anywhere
           it can be facing you
                        only as you look
with the late-year blues for
                a mean harvest echo
sent to sound our future
                in a chamber of its unfolding
not vaporous gnostic
            stuff with
bile from the gut
        we strip down to a vacancy

Let blood from our calendar
                void to the core
where the word has no voice
                a desolation
                      wailing to assert
where it was I went
            and what did I do
                    to see you go the other way

I so did not want to see any

                        light fail to guide our

muted exultation

                into ecstasy of

                       deprivation

                              one way out

Look ahead, as in retrospect. Say what you may but whatever the anguished prospect you came out of I'll know where I stand for the moment though the inner landscape refuses to bloom. Here winter flattens everything pallid to the ground so leveled it's cast and raised above a tarred gravel with the prospect blocked into reciprocal caves to left and right each one arched like a willing ear though deaf to the howling inside the hollow still echoes a buffered window shut on a blackness not even the blind can see through

Otherwise I'd have nothing to say

End Note

We see it's here, a sheen of polish
to close the year

Cold foresight now
will seal a liberating vow
with cheers the bells cut loose
to clear the view into the new
on an uncertain spark of promise
let's hope holds true

Enough, for Forrest Gander

The victim never being asked
to speak a word still can risk
abstinence to suit one's
own random occasion

Not let it go only so far
as the eye reaches

For each word to show dark value
froth of bitterness hardly there
from an unfathomed overflow
grief blends into contriving
the single line you intend

For what the prospect defines
mystery one word at a time
though it has a light
                              wayward glancing
by which to catch
struggle enacted for blunt fact
solitary is the joke of it
                              all as if

Wrestling to ungnarl a bunched up
secret known to all forever now
remembered more vaguely
                              Forgive
my drift into a rhetoric I was raised

to depend on with faith to ensure
the passing inertia in song

Gated Reverb from Lost '60s Film

Only so much you might say in

                        decent conversation

on a day like this how the wind

                        tries to send skimpy snowflakes

whichever way but only once

                        to where you worked on the drill

to kill with a clean conscience

                        taken for granted before with no name

every injustice comes to harm

                        even before you take aim at random

shadows jump into the frame

                        disguised to slip into a faulty

harassed lateshift worktime

                        now needs to be reclassified

where luck let each outtake

                        get drastic too much for

snowflakes folding into a

                        severe mold for much

more a shining moonlit

                        shield of insouciance

Welcoming

Come in and take your skin off, set down your load of bones.
Relax those feet, off at the ankles.

And the hands, careful!
Loosen each finger a little first.

That scalp with the ears? Toss it down anywhere
next to the head, another weight off your shoulders.

I see you brought a smile along, as usual.
Does it go with those teeth?

Your lungs there among the plants are doing fine.
Your heart too, not a vein out of place.

Sex? Doesn't matter.
Wrap that in with the bowels if you have to.

Now then, doesn't it feel easier?
And we like to see you as you really are.

13 Nov 15 Paris Time

So now all of a sudden
      rage is incendiary
you may never know
      we were human once
imagination fails
      when no one can explain
nightfall all too
      abruptly the truth of what
we become

No need to bury the past
      it does its own
      damage control
with the worst of it
      a momentary freeze
      the instant you're gone
your eye on the stars
      and each star a gun
      burst into blinding
slow vertigo of the long fall
      drilled into you once
      for no one to share
who can hold your hand
      when the same stabbing pain
      tears a hand from the gun
like an overwound clock
      on the instant or
      an overturned train

letting pain bleed
                    leaves all the facts barren
                    the worst that can happen
broken down
to the bone
            with no one left
            you forget your name

Never to believe it could ever happen
                                        not without some key
                                        benefit of reprisal
though it's happened before
                            no consoling phase
                            for relief yet to come
                            whatsoever

The clocktower stands
                        to sound the next hour
streets are swept clean
                        for the dance to resume
and all called to prayer
                            for another new turn
a scathing keen aim
                    failed to abort
the evening clears
                    too late to wake us
bullets can wait
            let the dead rest

Redoubt (Collioure)

From having been where painters used to
go harvesting their long views then

watch the waves return to churn up
foam for a sore-eyed chump like me

who knows just where the gods sprang from
but here I hear their beauteous undertaking

work wonders whispering to me a lingo from
just before I'd come to think the words could mean

more than I know or let on so the furtive stars
spark their glint from the same brightness

slamming in blind to airbrush the plain wave or
leave as lame a target as any human can

ever be ready for refusing death a welcome
inscrutably rude and green a springtime turn

from the get go and all solid waves to come

Torn Piece, Anselm Hollo in Memory

No kind of fervor
                even snapped from the sky
                                could so move us
to bind together a sleeve for all we lose
        as the hour tolls your going
to frame in mind a fading hymn to peace

Yank down the banner
                    where swallows cavort
                              scissoring
veils in a late haze only too frail to configure
ever so discreetly or discriminate from the swarm
muted whiffs of artillery in the blur
        of these cloud puffs
        so night never fails

You traced signs everywhere clear in detail
with a humor tenderly ironic
to spot the crow in what you saw
        for one you knew only too well
        but didn't get to know after all
had struck a bargain in blood
before the lights went

Every dream has a lookout
all eyes open wide
            as the child's
        on hearing language plain spoken

You left us to learn

First Light, among Crows

I go up the road and what do I see
a house with a car and a broken tv

some touch-toe birch deep in second growth
scrapped rusted cars past overgrown gravestones

host to a small congregation of huge black crows
their eyes fierce glinting midnight the other side

of a fence I came to once one high summer
the rhythm of late afternoon cradled oval shadows

in the flat middle of a deep mountain pond
your hair takes its sheen straight from the sun

so while that face holds your smile
a canoe I stand up in

while I limp you are the first light
your hands so small I see you wave

from a stage landscape I didn't need to dream
turns the blowtorch up to a cutting beam

Wall Piece, for Tony Long

10 nov 89 houseplants are fighting for air
In the ongoing struggle nighttime takes cover
An eclipse bans lightning from the sky
While blindness flares the roots

Forever means never now we have no cover
A swerve of raindrops takes to the pond
Some smarting dialog between lifelong pals

On the art of lost causes over a loss of authority
Skipping stones in all directions while the traffic
Begins to resemble a thickening sky
Incessant absence the common fear

No gauge to tell which one of us is younger
Words will snap back to nab the wise guy
With no release to reverse the ties that bind us

⤳

Steve Lacey played live taps on the green at Pere Lachaise
Your ashes left a pale trail washed off with the Paris broadcast
You'd caught live late in '91 the prelude Putsch to civil war at Tbilisi
Your seven sculptures rubbled in front of Georgian Parliament

Languages you picked up as readily as girls the Lithuanian at first
From friendship German then Russian as an army ration in the Tyrol
Farmers took you in and fed you when they found you asleep on their
    lawns

Then French when you signed on with one gallery
Metallic sculptures to grace public spaces with steel
Carved into a stable silence each sale
An advance on material costs and some loans
Put to a test that wrecked friendship for good

The last time you talked was by phone from a Paris hospital
A doctor came in and cut you off for good

Along the Roman Road

When traffic stalls
        you'll fail to see
                any mountains
in sublunar chalk
        for the blue bristle
                furze of hovering vapors
a tree stands bare
        where sheep once grazed
                like laundry
dropped from the line
        an itch is there to explore
                rare exploits
a brilliant future foiled here
        once then revived
                the graven
miracle in religion
        given another form
                could be your world
new to step into
        so what if nothing
                looks different from
what you can imagine
        home to be like
                not even close
strapped to a tree was
        depetalled here
                once and ever since

Nighttime, after Büchner, with a Postscript

One more night's come down on
Earth's old eternal globe
Just as darkness once more clots
A smokefilled dungeoncell's throat

P. S. *from an unknown German source*:
I live with a Body flailing wildly for Spirit
                    to be more in the Living

Jonas Mekas at 90

Our fields stay open
to the sun's charge
late harvest claim
a growing snow
-borne quiet

You make
the night go
your own way
suspend in time
a word you find

And crack
the sweet
illumination
open on
itself

So extra
-ordinary from
the inside out
as outside in

To signify a world
we haven't seen
or heard of yet

Secured at every
nomination of
the breath

In lifelong song

Almanach Citation for This Late A Date

Head thrown back to shake some memory loose
       the silence a steady radio static
Nothing stays open this late
       and I've run out of friends to call at this hour
The book face down, and I'm no Artaud
       but it's this plus sleepless till dawn can make
       an eerie trailer for plum horror show
Clock's early alarm rumbling for the world
       like a subway deep underground

It's hard to say just what I may have in mind
       right now it should be winter with a light snow
       everywhere on show locks you in so you have to squint
Though it almost looks back at you nowhere so bright
       while a slow corrosion inside the bone
       perks to surface with your name
Before it drowns in my blood

Until the smallest silent pause between words
       suddenly heavy with loss lets me know how
       gravity works its routine to recharge the way
Winter weather will block everything in
       for each tree to trace a separate network
       of scars lightning might have left
So it's back to the roots
       which always stay dark
       an uneasy trap into sleep

Snowflakes pillowed her mind
      pale with embers to quarter a moon
On footsteps along the pebbled shore

Birds in my feathers
      she'd said from the pillow

Birds to sing

Words for a Head, for Bill Polyn

his Drawing, 1971

Sure it spins, the world
on my shoulders, so if
I lean in, I can see
me dizzy, double
though one eye's patched
on a satellite's track
over the drift
of my face.

Hey man, here goes! Hair
fins out in a wing, one ear strains
to point direction, as
from the prop of a mustache
the nose lifts, and the head
takes off!

After years of heavy
breathing
and trying to keep
the weight square
on these shoulders

I'm almost
up there,
in a sphere
of pure decorum,

where my undershirt,
buttoned,
won't keep me out
and the twin
antipodes (goatee
and Katzenjammer curl)
pass muster.

That's
far out!

Ptume

It has to be mad transgressive to say the least

Ptume

To say there is nothing to saying what there is

Ptume

Before origin or simply put before sound

Ptume

Imagination haunts a silence etymologica figura cannot redeem

Ptume

The word is already a ready concretization of echoes

Ptume

A stone in the roadbed is memoryprone you might say

Ptume

More or less

Ptume

The Lovers Before Us

for Lygeia Grace and Bill Crozier
13 feb 99

At the busy crossroads where a solitary statue
like my uneasy self regards pigeons and cars
so now a wintry day flares into a fixed gaze
as seasons wheel on to bring our late show
an indeterminate blink closer to extinction

But when love takes priority spring comes early
and the lovers before us take us by surprise
in sharing the wonder children are wise to
in spite of grown-ups who may cry that marriage
is no mirage to build on wishes and live in dreams

Time will not let them stand like statues
however far they go and whatever they find there
holding to each other as the heart holds to life
they will feel at home and as long as they are together
know that love is always more than anyone can remember

Flag Down

It snaps in the wind
like a dog at heels
and flaps like a hand
singed or chilled.
Like a slap
it startles and is very dramatic.

Let's face it, to salute
it means about as much
as turning the other cheek.
It is, and is not, done in real life.

Many still disregard as routine
its climb to the top
and dismiss the occasional
dip to half-mast.
And many have died for it.

Now look, how it lifts at the head of the parade
sharp as a drumsnare.
And fits the coffin like a glove.

It will climb mountains,
scaling peaks wherever there are mountains,
and must climb where there are none,
a design for crawling men.

When there's no air to breathe:
eyes up, aim low!

Burning, it rages into shreds and turns another color,
an ornery thing turned on itself, trying to hide,

slack at last, blackened to ash.

Forked Uplift

Near as the grass
is I still can't
feel it

Nothing
it says is
as good as

The first breeze
echoes
fruit and wood

The world I feel
holds sunlight
then

The sun shifts

A Song for & from Rene Ricard

You had a song to sing
                    and lived the song
Your days still haunt us
                    as nights are long
Days run too short so
                    night never ends
To turn all the many
                    odd characters friends
Solid enough to declare
                    Love's victory
Your best queer wish
                    at the temple of flesh

Lapse to Reprieve

When the longest night gains on our shortest
the groan next door won't let me sleep either

Waiting around with
                    time to think only
                    about getting out

So want the curse to
                    lift from each shadow
                    and anchor the dream

A pure joy language is
                    meant to uncover
                    for our sake invest

So much more
than a laugh can carry

These Days. An Essay in Real Time

... who emigrates except to be better off?
Melville: *Pierre, or The Ambiguities*

Strangers will amuse themselves at your expense
their hands and tongues may not yet be tied
but you still feel a whiplash these days

We call them aliens and take away their cards
though scars fail to congeal in torture cells
so let the overcrowding sort them out

If you hope to build yourself up
flaunt open wounds with no scabs
on spec for 15-min glamor stats

But while that's not yet the case
you may have been hearing
of a fast retreat to the islands

Just don't let them go
from Guantanamo

❧

"After the big fight of last Friday night
I still picture the lump on Joe Louis's shoulder
dark as the specter of Stalin in a gray resolution
        on the TV at the neighbors' downstairs

"I could never cue into at will until the kid got quizzed
on Bach's Gloria and I knew the answer too
still keeping in mind the trickle runoff a brilliant
        rainbow from industrial oilslick and all that

"Way before Iran got slammed by the CIA poor wellaimed
wily radical Mosadegh dumped for the oil but who knew
what with Grace Kelly around we'd only
        put up with a front that was royal"

        ❧

They'll say that for those left behind
unbereaved where you are not wanted
what it means merely to survive
by now through a curdled reprieve
in wasting the surplus from some ancient haul
now you have no recourse except to play it safe
enshrined with a bold marker to a blasted place
in a shade impenetrable and ghastly fierce
having figured on no firm grasp
how to scalp a bald man
the first time you see him
in these hairy precincts

        ❧

shed primitive perceptions
initiate a scolding ritual
blunt and direct never to
leave anyone undone

a gloss on oblivion
leadens redemption
biological nonsense
from crib to coffin

by the logic of nonsense

not one bit
for an obit

❧

"That boy behind the shed give him a slice of cheese
an apple and he's quiet the whole night
so long the horse don't lean in
with lips
        thick to snap it up
just like that
          that summer
"Bombs keep falling like apples in autumn
but only that one night we crept in
under the house into the half-cellar"

❧

what it means to replenish a rundown
stall with minced metallic shards
in the narrow shallows of a trough
left over to catch a clean nosedive
with no preliminary cash-in from
renegotiation let alone a rehearsal
built into a history so unrepentant

it's twisted sad beyond all grief
with no rest for the bereaved

And they say of people moving
to cooling northern islands
they escape some irrepressible
erotic pull
to take its toll in dollars spent
on their routinely cautionary
urban isolation

     ~

"Wally it's not the dead end of the world we feel
at the sight of a napalmed palmtree
let the butt of each spine sit cushioned and quake
       while there is war going on
to spare us from pursuing a new myth without Kafka
       the ring of conspiracy we can drown in"

     ~

It was a darn good while before they got out
Not a long while but a while
It was good they got out before they found
Themselves embedded in the habit

     ~

Fire has one element
firepower scorching
all consuming means
newspaper dosages

tie an eye to rumor
as the only witness
to survive the draft

　　　～

Though the face shows we'll have to
　　　　　　　call up something else
a remnant
　　　renegade
　　　　　　　trusted friend
　　　　　　　nor settle for less
so worn down
　　　　　　proud as the hour
　　　　　　shapes our sleep
while flags get torn
　　　　　　her lipstick binge
　　　　　　brings a hip-turn
minefield silence
　　　　　　summertime spring
what all now shows
　　　　　　on the air even when
　　　　　　against the odds we clamor
for something else
　　　　　　losing ourselves so far for
　　　　　　not having said enough
while the war goes on someplace else

　　　～

"I wish that my old friend Tony was here he so
much wanted to hear how they flew the bombs in

90

"He wanted to become a pilot so he boned up hours
on Civil Air Patrol and watched those skies fully alert

"What he really wanted was to fly away and he did"

～

No war can be worse
                                        than the one right now
where the killings
                                        take place media-blitzed
morbid nightcode
                                        clear as rain
                                                                drumming the roof
right when you drop
                                        with no keen feeling
                                                                                left
to charge or march on
                                        the limbs loosen
                                                                        and fold
just as all the pain
                                        gets numbed to numberless

～

Those bloodlet beauties
                                        have gone where the centuries
can no longer reach
                                        then return without posturing
fame for a name
                                        till there's no gain to the blame

Don't listen to this
                    if you had your last wish
get lost in the processing
                    time after time
yet to speak with the dead
                    you have only to listen
beforehand
          for a blanching
ripe fire before sundown
                    sure to let you know
it can't be slowed down
                    or stowed hid
from gawkers who'd endorse
                    your fears
even when you can't share them
                    left alone
to eat your knuckle-sandwich
                    only solid
     leaves no clue
                    meanwhile
just wait
          for the call
                    to be served some smooth
     nonsequitur

Crusoe's Comeback

Words still come through
not mine though I'll say
what I could've been up to

If you must know
there has to be life
to ease the thread

Now I've grown old
not a clue to what wind
turns the face of each day

Afresh each season
and that gladly yes
I'm ready to unfold

What I own that's gold
all yours to find it's
no longer mine

Brave brooder
take my word
not all the tale's been told

Axial Radar, for George Quasha

Each premise is cordial
                          and clear as a handprint
Time bound and trying hard
                             hand to hand stack
Hard as rock touch distilled
                          tied to its scale
Time tells a warped tale
                         crowded as a history
Reft of all flesh a bell
                        abrasive human mold
With weight at worst
                     wired to a hairline
Rage from a light
                -ning perch at each seam
A bruise fold
              heft in the heartbeat
It takes two
              to the same place it stays
To claim
          a balance beyond all control
In this
        one dream
                no one is a stranger

Evening into Meaning

For an eager guide to sunrise
each look has the summons
surprise you sometime

Shadow the web of lost intrigue
still dipped in the flair
of sheer misconception

Evening into meaning with
the hope of a happier future
for our shell-shocked planet

Later Last Night

Funny to think of
        how a gabled room
in a summer house glows
        a palm vivid noon
I open the door and go in
        not sure I've been
here before though it's a
        nice kind of a quiet
empty snug eyrie the kids
        my own two now
just the right age could
        stay in and play
I'm here to check out
        then see a glum
blotch parked like a
        moth not
sure it's dead or not
        on an otherwise
spotless wall the sure
        precaution I take
approaching eyes open
        broomstick in hand
I can trap with and not
        crush the suspect
but focus on and want to
        show my kids even
thinking as I tense my
        wrist to jab

though not quick
            enough as this
thing unhinges its
            whirring bat
wings its flimsy
            circling
I'm in dread of
            tracking
now never get to
            show kids
it's a hovering
            powerhouse
fist all set to get
            anyone so
suddenly strange a
            bloated nearly
translucent giant of
            a guppyfish
drifts in to gulp up
            all the gloom
and I blink

One Sky, for Kenny "Angel" Davis

a vast memorial the clouds storm past

the dream of stars
a trail of cinders
            the knifeline
            a lifetime
                        of the few
                        who knew
    in close formation
    slow walks on
                crushed gravel
                rockets outblast
                            grinding to
                            incineration
got me in the eye once
                too close to where
            it was
                        all day long
                        getting dark
a wind through the walls
            spoke of nothing
                    as usual
    the last a rest room
                        time couldn't erase its worst feature
                        while each day offers the same excuse

        Day 2 into his Age of Reason
        June 17 has our own boy raging: "You're not

boss of the whole
world & I don't
have to do anything
you say"

Under a corroding tin lid
waist-deep in regrets, stalled
in the inner workings
But where'd you ever find
the moment choice, if not
in each other's arms, that moment's
smoldering
under a dome
HERE
LOVE
LIES
all huddling together
as the mudslide began
hands and face coated
ash saturates the air

I hope
it was not
God said
one neighbor
drowned in the torrent
ash and rainwater
downed telephone lines
impassable roads
101 died

killed outright
homes down highrise
collapse

hundreds go missing
hundreds of thousands
and more left homeless
the other side of the world, via NYTimes
TUESDAY, June 18
Enter at peril, you do not live here
High Court 5–4 has
Elderly Poor Paying
Defining People by Race
Billions
Too Much

Refugees Describe Horror

Lawsuits on Prison Cruelty

6,OOO
Layoff
Notices
Male-Only Policy
Disgruntled, in Low Turnout

Doomsday
Exhumed

I'm the man inside, the main job, the fire inside mind's firetrap

one woman sleeps here
one found a warm spot
cement sleeping floor
door opens & looks in

surprised not one bit
though all unexpected
one woman shows care
one woman watches TV
her heart bare in her face
one woman smiles sleepy
dreams one'll never forget
or get up in time for
 BREAK GLASS
 a la Russe IN CASE OF
 FIRE

 Iguana prize pintsize
 rubberized housepet
 dawn's easy herald
 painted kidproof
 colors
Things do look different
where the shiver of a river
is a scaly skin tongue flick
fiery glint in the roving eye
 Things to do different
 if not by the numbers
to work for a living
 recall my wins
 reveal mistakes
take a break & a breather, whenever
I'm thinking, have fears I may take
a loss can't be faked
 deliver the goods

wrap it to chuck

                 all away

        end it

       and yet

      Fear glints reflected in the nutty eye

sidewalk apostle on the primal draw

finds winter depopulated

Let me tell you about the night

Intuition guides all

      the way to China

          think Ai WeiWei   Even today

shorn of color   bereft at sunrise   (thinking Ai WeiWei)

Places you've been just don't

       feel the same   thank Ai WeiWei

    Your face at the window   Bliss it was to be there

    No match for the bargain   Nostalgia comes ragged

    That our nights together   A stand-in vacuum in space

    Torched before we touched Where to point the hour

And leave before   choke on broken debris

      fate seals off all hope

    the crock once held flowers

A stray din sprayed too thin and too soon to regret   26 may

                  TO FORTIFY

    Tool around this room & tumble

out into daylight

                    rumpled like
        fresh laundry flesh that's just
        had time to find the sun trundle
                    dry to fortify
                at the head
            an emblematic
dream that came
Instead

        Once, in the Movies (More than Once)

then, & then, &
                Then Some
                                        Ritual of the Ring (unannointed)
Consumatum Non Est (honest)

            let it rest, so
                    let it rot

                                    rustic & quaint, the bones of it left
                                    gloss on the rigor, bared to flyswarms
                                                giving incorruptible
                                    Patience a bad name, rank net & gross
                                    web of insecurity, dropping & reaching
                                                no basis whatsoever

Hic Jacet   straitjacket   "come to this"

        Dancing   & dancing   & dancing

                              breaks, crack-web'd
                 Smashed
                 in the
          Mirrors
          A storm

     an[d]
     End

Concurrency

Otillia
my
Otillia

In 9th grade it was
I had such a crush on you

From the second seat in front
I'd watch you sashay into Home Room

Every schoolday we shared
a couple of classes and our mutual interest

kept me from revealing my immigrant lowlife
while you were a well-to-do Jew

after Anonymous Sanskrit

I miss your kiss
           Heaven sent bliss

A shiver of rain
           to ease the strain

A balm of kindness
           in shared reminders

Too much is lost
        at human cost

Love so unique
        seldom comes cheap

Where is the Snow They Promised

Where is the snow they promised?

The leaves are off the tree, after their fire

The branches splayed, despoiled, their frayed fervor

Fixed a casual sign against the sky

To open wide on quietude, its meditative gray

Color of my mind, inert as the arrogance

Of my crazy-eyed self mounts a back residue

Assigned this morning to quench all sunlight

Scorch and subdue the smoke-choked chimneys

Absorbing all into a meaningless loopy silence

But is it worth to wait the while, let wonder

Take charge where my heart can't handle it

No more

All as if, by Another Light

For mere millennia we've had the centuries unfold
lost in space whether we know it not giving us hope
though hope still extending far with a universal aim
overlooking any gain from a closer inspection

So it's all been said. though
you haven't heard the half of it
and yet

You
        are all
That
        there is

Go and we will
where it's too late
for language

So before what it was

Watch it waken and walk

Sol Invicta
what the Roman once said

You can't beat the sun
now that we get the daylight
beat out of us

So it was that I saw before me his slow Ghost approaching from a hol-
low that was not quite the cave I had imagined at all but ready to be fit
to a meaning: as though to have been awake before even being aware of
The Monster inside for the very allure of rattled preconception would
leap out to startle prayerfully your eminence into spearhead for conver-
sation; an isolationist tactic, not meant to evolve ...

as slimy thought slinks into misconceived tautology
that has no bearing here

Brecht broke the rule, but did he stay in character?
"Don't say tomorrow it may never come ,,,
Why think of sorrow when you're having fun?"

The first thing I'd have to say is the word *travaill* in Elizabethan days
had 2 meanings, at least: trek and work. Shakespeare gives it both ways.

> Weary with toyle, I hast me to my bed,
> The deare repose for lims with trauaill tired,
> But then begins a iourny in my head
> To worke my mind,when boddies work's expired.
>
> *Sonnet 27*

And so far all that tells us is figurative. The travel could be from his
kind, a writer setting out to rest up after a being worn out by a ful-
ly committed engagement on his writing project. The 'iourny' that
prompts comes from a memory. Maybe unprompted, but by a simple
shift, the 'worke' being mechanical, but 'thoughts' come as a qualifier,
drifting into a committed tour of 'pilgrimage' to what would be *perhap*
A Dream of San Francisco if I'd ever been where it uncoils the mantra
of belonging; but back to this Shakespeherian

Looking on darkness which the blinde do see
but as it would be savoring rather than saving this sight (not even
insight, just a fluctuation that happens, inwardly, maybe) so that we
(rather) have it register as

... a iewell,(hung in ghastly night)
Makes blacke night beauteous
And so it ends, if we take it for what it is, a desperate continuation of
the struggle all dedicated writers should be engaged in, for this is over
all a dedicatory sonnet to himself, the author, finding a way to extend
the journey, himself or herself, going on to 'love what you are doing'and
that's all that fits. It's a kind of exasperation without reprieve possibble,
a mindbend into uncertwin futurity.

... noe quiet finde.
is the signoff.
And ther, if we would want to, it ends; but should we go on, and I don't
mean the following sonnet (which shifts gears, anyway) I could only
continue with a poem, a poem of my own, the way haiku invites one to
continue on the thought suggested, so you could add on and apply, not
necessarily to advance, the suggestion on inference further, so that there
it be, unconfirmed, unmolested, the way you want it to be:

Mea canto
flouredescantingly yours, or mine if I want it to be eflourescent, prodi-
giously yours, take it or leave it, not mine alone, so let it be unmolested
Australian, where they go to breathe and recover
if they can and not just because they've become exhausted or taken
in by renegotiations of the primal palaver, that is yours Doll (and you
asked for it) as I see you tomorrow at breakfast, which will never come,
though I may wish for it, withouth you, it never is an outcome

Let it rest within an advisory capacity, where I found YOU a figment,
even in letting become a fragment of outercommencing incertitude
(where I've been, & who's gonna stop me?) BELIEVE ME and there it
was a radical take-off into a field of resistance that only the French ever
saw a pusilanimous ponderance that the French ever beleaguared as the
saying goes beleaguered by its aristhismoees (& soitgoes) fermented for
its youth

Right
    now
You
    are that
All
    there is

If at All

Where the word leads
is no guidance
we have been there before
if at all
over again beyond doubt
whether the ice will melt
with the corpses snug in the harbor

What you were spared could not have happened
the voice of the dead was a cutting wind

Each letter shakes on its stem while the root has a climber

They stood in the small stand of woods like the trees
with suitcases packed
and were any still alive we'd remember

While sitting on the hilltop
I kept watching the stars
with darkness a cold wind
kicked straight in my eyes
that carried the somber pinegrove's song
down to all sleeping humankind

And was it just that
                    time went by

Or maybe death
                    itself went with it

I wanted to clear my mind of everything
but the mind played this trick

if I could only
remember

Colors faded with assorted voices
that was when I first closed my eyes

and the blur was astonishing

The next thing that happened
before it had ever been

the first news the war had ended

and not been there either

that the sun the moon the stars kept me spellbound
and that had been the one wish

only to tear the letter with the invitation
open with my teeth

new ponds the fish no longer swim in
while coins devalue as they sink in the brine

slowmotion spin
                   with the sun no longer
                                    losing its sheen

Odds

Once we seal this envelope let it be for the future
Let anxiety leave its tang crude as autumn
Area codes consumer bar codes
Just so there's justice on the sleeve
To lift the odds swept you in

Or was it the fitting slippers
Carried you into my comfort zone
Made you stride crisply unimpeded

As all doors open for you
By the shield you wear
Freshly endowed
Luminous smile

Morgana Selva

The one that I knew a gem
                of a blonde
The time I saw she was
                running natural
                gave no clue
The time I saw she was
                talking with a guy
                we both knew
The time I saw she was
                rapt to listen
                for what was new
The time I saw she was
                in the cafeteria
                talking movies
The time I saw her what
                caught my eye held
                more than the view
The time I saw her was
                with or without her
                all I would lose
The time I saw her was
                a breakthrough
                no way too close
The time I saw her was
                the very last time
                too late to hold

Once More

To have survived
              the chokehold of night
                            "unto the Day"
is almost to say
              the surfeit of light
                        has that rare
prayer to share in
              a chorale
                    to awaken and lift us
              before later doings weigh in
to dim and diminish
                  with a daring enough
                  abrupt to give in to
plain human display

About the Author

PHOTO: SUSAN QUASHA

VYT BAKAITIS has published four books of poems, including *con/structs*, a book of visual poems and photographs (limited edition, Arunas K. Photo+Graphics, NYC). He recently completed *The Antigone Play*, adapted from Sophocles by way of Hölderlin's renowned German version, and is currently editing *Transcience: or, Exile Tours*, his assorted readings in lyric poetry from various cultures. Bakaitis' many works of translation include four books of original poems by renowned filmmaker Jonas Mekas, as well as *XL Poems* by Julius Keleras (Spuyten Duyvil, 2002). He recently edited *Message Ahead: Poets Respond to the Poems of Jonas Mekas* (Rail Editions, 2019). Bakaitis is a native of Lithuania and has lived since 1968 in New York City.